REDSTONE

HACKS FOR
MINECRAFTERS

TABLE OF CONTENTS

Redstone is one of the most amazing and complicated aspects to Minecraft. With it you can invent brand-new, working in-game machines, from an automatic door to a flying machine or calculator. Some of the most popular contraptions to make are:

- Automatic farms, to help harvest crops

- Mob farms, to gather and kill large numbers of mobs and get their drops

- Automatic doors

- Automatic lighting

- Item sorting and storage

Where Do You Get Redstone?

You get redstone by mining redstone ore at levels 16 and lower. Each block of ore will get you 4 or 5 redstone, and more if you are mining with a Fortune-enchanted pick. Witches sometimes will drop redstone when they die, and priest villagers may also trade it.

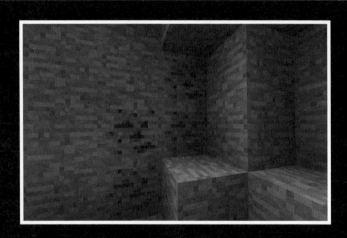

Redstone machines, or contraptions, have three main elements: devices, power, and the signal that transmits power to the device. A redstone device is an object that performs an action when it receives power. Redstone power comes from specific power source blocks, such as redstone blocks and torches. You can extend the reach of this power through trails of redstone dust.

Here is the one of the simplest redstone contraptions, a trap-door activated by a button.

This trapdoor is activated by a button on the next block.

The power source is the button, which gives out a temporary power signal when it is pressed. While that signal exists, the trapdoor opens. When the signal disappears, the trapdoor closes. You don't need any redstone dust if the power source is right against the device. However, if you want the button to be farther away from the trapdoor, you would have to connect the trapdoor and the button through redstone dust.

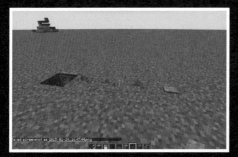

This button is placed farther away from the trapdoor, so you use redstone dust to carry its signal.

The best way to understand redstone is to learn by doing. When you read about the devices in the first three chapters, play around and hook them up together to see what happens. When you make one of the projects and it works, make it again and add your own changes to see what works and what doesn't.

Redstone dust and devices like torches, repeaters, and comparators can be uprooted by water, destroying contraptions. Make sure when you finish a contraption to protect it from accidental water placement by walling it off.

It is much easier to start learning redstone in Creative mode, where you have access to all items to play with. If you don't, each project has a complete list of components so you can gather these before beginning.

Placing blocks and items for a contraption can sometimes be tricky. In the projects, in order to place a block in a certain location, you may need to first place other temporary blocks that the first block can rest on. You'll want to remember to remove any temporary blocks, so it can help to choose a specific type of material for these blocks, like red wool.

Sometimes to place objects, like hoppers, on top of others, you may need to shift-right-click (holding the shift button while right-clicking). Some objects always place to face you (like pistons). You may need to move around a bit, or place some temporary blocks to stand in the right place, in order to place these correctly.

Use a special block, like red wool, for temporary blocks you use to stand on or to help place objects. This will help you remember to remove them later.

If you complete a project, but it isn't working the way you think it should, go through the steps to check if everything is in place and pointing in the right direction. Important first things to check when a contraption doesn't work include:

- Are repeaters, comparators, and redstone dust pointing in the right direction?

- Are any blocks being powered that shouldn't be?

- What isn't receiving power that should be?

- Is a redstone torch turning off a signal?

- Should any repeaters have delays?

Many of the contraptions in this book are based on mechanisms that other Minecraft players have created and shared online, in forums, or on video-sharing sites like YouTube. Making contraptions following other people's designs is a great way to start understanding redstone. However, you will start to understand even more when you take these contraptions apart, and put them back again slightly differently, to figure out exactly how they work.

Note: This book's projects were created in Minecraft 1.8.1 for PC and updated to reflect Minecraft 1.13 redstone capabilities. If you are playing with a different version of Minecraft, you may find some differences. For the latest information on a device or item, check the Minecraft Wikipedia, at Minecraft.gamepedia.com.

CHAPTER 1

REDSTONE POWER

For a redstone contraption to work, there must be a source of power or redstone signal. Some power sources send power constantly, like redstone torches. Other sources only emit power when they are turned on, like a switch. Some, like buttons, may only send a redstone signal for a short period of time.

Power sources send power to themselves (the block space they are in) and also, usually, to the blocks they are attached to. Different power source items have slightly different rules about what blocks (or block spaces) they send power to.

Some power sources also power the blocks *next to* the block they are attached to. These include buttons, detector rails, levers, pressure plates, and tripwire hooks. Your main power sources will be redstone torches, redstone blocks, buttons, and levers.

A redstone torch provides power constantly, to itself and to the block above it. It will provide power to attached redstone dust, repeaters and comparators, and attached redstone devices like pistons. (The repeaters must be facing away from the torch, as this devices receives signals from the back. Comparators receive signals from the side or back.) A redstone torch doesn't provide power to the block it is placed on. In fact, if the block the redstone torch is on receives power from another block or source, the redstone torch will turn *off*.

Redstone torch recipe.

Redstone Blocks

A redstone block is another power source that is always on. Unlike a torch though, it can't be turned off. It powers redstone dust, comparators, repeaters, and most redstone devices above, below, or around it, like doors or redstone lamps. The exception is a piston, which cannot be activated if the power source is directly in front of it.

Redstone block recipe.

Levers

A lever provides a constant power source when it is turned on. When you place a lever, it is in the off position. It provides power to the block it is on, and any attached redstone dust or devices.

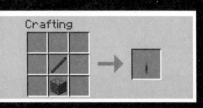

Lever recipe.

Observer

An observer is a redstone component that will produce a redstone pulse when it sees a change in the state of the block right in front of it. The front of the observer is the observing side with the face. The back shows a small circular outlet, which flashes red when it emits a pulse.

The observer has a worried-looking face on its front, an arrow pointing to the back on its top, and a little light on its back.

Block state changes are changes to characteristics of a block that are stored in data about that block. A melon stem growing from stage 1 to stage 2 is an example of a block state change. The block itself is still a melon stem, but one characteristic--its growth stage--has changed. The observer sees almost all block state changes, with a few exceptions. In 1.13 Java edition, exceptions include: opening and closing chests, beacons activating, item frames being placed, and sugar cane grown by bonemeal.

Observer recipe.

Buttons

Buttons can be made of either stone or wood, and they provide power only for a short time. A stone button will send power for 1 second, while a wood button will send power for 1.5 seconds. (One exception is if an arrow hits a wood button, the arrow will keep the button pressed until the arrow despawns or is picked up.) Buttons power the block they are on and any attached redstone dust or devices.

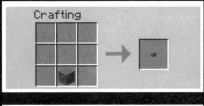

Wood button recipe.

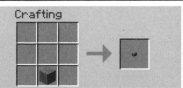

Stone button recipe.

Pressure Plates

Like buttons, pressure plates provide temporary power and are made of stone or wood. Stone or wood pressure plates provide power for 1 second, or for the time an item or entity is on it. Pressure plates are activated by players, mobs, or a minecart with a mob in it. Wooden plates can also be activated by arrows, fishing rod lures, any minecart, and any dropped items. A pressure plate powers the block beneath it, and any attached redstone dust or devices.

Wood pressure plate recipe.

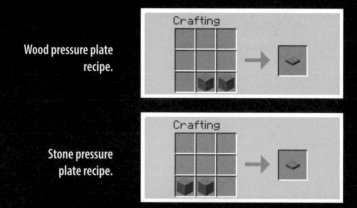

Stone pressure plate recipe.

Weighted Pressure Plates

Weighted pressure plates are similar to regular pressure plates but are made of either gold or iron. They are different from regular pressure plates only in the strength of signal they produce. Their signal depends on the number of mobs or items on top of them. The light (gold) pressure plate gives out a signal strength equal to the number of mobs, up to 15. So 8 items on the plate will make it send out a signal for 8 blocks, and 16 will make it send out a signal of 15 blocks. The heavy (iron) plate needs many more mobs to give increased signal strength. It will only reach the full 15-block-long strength when more than 140 mobs are on it.

Weighted pressure plate (light) recipe.

Weighted pressure plate (heavy) recipe.

Detector Rails

A detector rail provides a power signal when a minecart is on it. It will power any attached redstone dust and devices, as well as the block it is on. Detector rails are often used to switch the tracks a minecart is on. If a minecart with a chest or hopper is on it, the detector rail will send a signal strength that shows how full that container is.

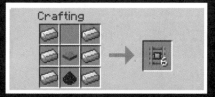

Detector rail recipe.

Tripwire Hooks

You can make a tripwire from two tripwire hooks connected with string. The two hooks power the blocks they are attached to when the string between them is stood on or walked over. They also provide power to attached redstone dust and devices. The two tripwire hooks can be up to 40 blocks apart.

Tripwire hook recipe.

Trapped Chests

Trapped chests provide power when they are opened to attached redstone dust and devices, as well as the block they are placed on. The power sent to redstone dust or the block will be the same as the number of players opening the chest, with a maximum strength of 15. Unlike many devices, however, they won't provide power to a comparator. A comparator can still measure the signal strength of a trapped chest.

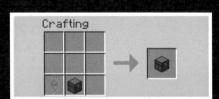

Trapped chest recipe.

Daylight Sensors

Daylight sensors activate in the presence of sunlight. The amount of power they provide depends on the strength of the sunlight, so during dawn their signal strength will rise upwards from 1 to a maximum of 15 during full sunlight. During sunset, their power decreases until there is no sunlight left. You can also invert a daylight sensor by right-clicking it. An inverted sensor does the opposite—the amount of power it provides depends on how little sunlight there is. That means the strength will increase the darker it gets. Daylight sensors are great objects for making redstone contraptions that turn on and off at certain times of the day, like automatic street lighting.

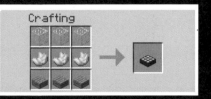

Daylight
sensor recipe.

Containers

Containers are items that can store things and have inventories. Brewing stands, chests, dispensers, droppers, furnaces, hoppers, and jukeboxes are all containers. They provide a power signal to a comparator. The strength of the signal depends on how full they are. A chest with 27 slots but only 3 items will send a weaker signal than a hopper with 5 slots and 3 items. How full they are also depends on the sizes of the stacks of the items they contain. A chest filled with eggs (which stack to 16) will send a stronger signal than a chest half filled with sticks (which stack to 64). Even though the second chest has more items, the first chest has used more of the potential space. One exception is the jukebox. The signal it sends out depends on which disc is in it; different discs have different strengths.

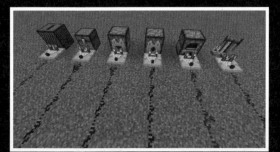

Containers
send signals to
comparators
showing how full
they are.

CHAPTER 2

REDSTONE DUST AND SIGNALS

You can power devices by placing the power source right next to the device, but you will often want to separate the two. To do this, you use redstone dust, which carries the power from source to device. Redstone dust that is carrying power sparkles and emits particles. If it is unpowered, there are no particles.

Redstone dust has some traits that can make moving a signal a bit tricky.

Redstone Dust Signals Only Travel 15 Blocks

Every block that redstone dust travels, the signal strength it carries decreases. The highest strength is 15, and the maximum distance redstone dust can carry a signal by itself is 15 blocks. This means that if powered redstone dust runs for two blocks, its strength at the end of those two blocks is 13, because 15 (the maximum power) minus 2 (the power it lost) is 13. You can change the length a redstone signal travels by using a device called a redstone repeater.

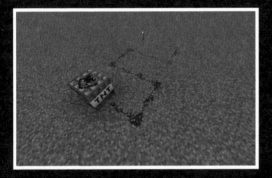

Redstone signal stops after 15 blocks.

Redstone Dust Can't Be Placed on All Blocks

You can't place redstone dust on most transparent blocks (blocks you can see through) like grass and glass, or stairs or slabs. However, you can put redstone on upside-down slabs, (slabs placed in the top half of a block space), on top of upside-down stairs, and on glowstone.

Redstone can't travel over bottom slabs or most transparent blocks. It can travel over upside-down (top half) slabs.

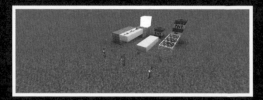

Redstone Dust Has to Be Placed Properly to Power a Device or Block

Redstone needs to point at a device or block in order to power it. If your trail of redstone dust travels by a device without pointing at it, it won't power that device. The exception to this is when you place just one single dot of redstone dust and it points nowhere. This can power blocks to all four sides.

This redstone dust powers only the dropper on the left.

This single dot of redstone dust is "directionless," because it's not pointing anywhere. It can transmit power to all sides, so all three of these droppers are powered.

Powered Opaque Blocks

Redstone dust powers the opaque blocks it is on and points to when it is active and lit up. (Opaque blocks are non-transparent blocks like stone, bricks, wool, etc.) A block powered by redstone dust is said to be weakly powered, because it doesn't have enough power to activate additional redstone dust next to it, on top of it, or under it. A block powered by a redstone power source or component, like a repeater or torch, is strongly powered. A strongly powered block can power redstone dust next to it. Both weakly powered and strongly powered blocks can activate redstone devices.

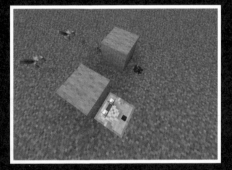

Here, redstone dust sends the same power to two blocks. These blocks are weakly powered— they have enough power to turn on an attached comparator (bottom) but not enough to turn on redstone (top).

Redstone Dust Can Only Travel 1 Block Vertically

To move redstone dust vertically more than one block, you need to use a staircase, so that it travels one block over for each block it rises. You can also use glowstone or upside-down slabs in an alternating pattern. Because these two blocks are both seen as transparent, they don't cut off the signal at the block edges where they touch.

Three ways of moving a signal up: Upside-down slabs (left), glowstone (middle), and a staircase (right).

A fourth alternative is to use redstone torches in an alternate pattern. Because these turn the signal off and then on, you have to be careful that the final torch is on to maintain the signal.

You can also alternate torches to move a signal up.

These methods only work for moving a signal up. To move a signal down, you will have to use a staircase or create a special contraption. You can make a spiral staircase that takes up less space.

A spiral staircase can move signals down (and up) in a small space.

Changing the Redstone Signal

There are two devices you can use to change the power of a signal traveling along redstone dust. These are the repeater and the comparator, and they are very important parts of many redstone contraptions.

Redstone Repeaters

The redstone repeater takes a redstone signal pointed to its back and refreshes it to the full 15 power level. This allows you to carry a signal farther than 15 blocks. At the fifteenth block or earlier, before the redstone fizzles out, place a repeater pointing in the direction the signal is moving. There's an arrow on the repeater that shows you which way it is pointing. There are also two mini-torches that light up when the repeater is powered.

The signal on the right is too long to reach the TNT. On the left, a repeater makes it happen.

Repeaters also can delay a signal. Traveling through a repeater delays the signal by 1 redstone tick. You can change this to a delay of 2, 3, or 4 ticks by right-clicking the repeater. When you do this, the back torch changes position to show the change in delay. Two other uses for repeaters are to maintain signal direction and to lock a signal. With complex redstone wiring, it often helps to use a repeater to make sure a signal is only going where you want it. And if you need for some reason to prevent a repeater's signal from changing, you can power it from the side to lock it. As soon as power from the side is removed, the lock is removed also.

Crafting

Repeater recipe.

What's a Redstone Tick?

A redstone tick lasts about one tenth of a second, and redstone contraptions measure and react to each other based on this unit of time. A redstone tick is twice the length of a game tick, which lasts one twentieth of a second. Game ticks are used in programming the game to measure and time events, like when plants grow.

Redstone Comparators

A comparator is a bit like a repeater, and it looks very similar, except it has three mini-torches on it instead of two. Like a repeater, it has an arrow on it that shows the direction it is pointing. It takes a signal coming in from the back and compares it to a signal coming in at its side. The comparator outputs a signal that is the same strength as the back signal, *unless* there is a side signal that has greater strength. Then the comparator will produce no signal. This is called comparison mode. (There can be two side signals, left and right.)

Redstone comparator recipe.

The front torch of this comparator is unlit, so you know it is in compare mode. The side signal is stronger (it's closer) than the back, so the comparator sends no signal out its front.

You can also put the comparator into subtract mode. To do this, right-click the comparator, and the front torch will light up. In subtract mode, the comparator will take the back signal strength, and subtract the greatest of any side signal. The signal it puts out is equal to the result. So if the strongest side signal is level 4, and the back signal is level 15, it will output a signal of level 11.

The comparator is in subtract mode here—the front torch is on. It subtracts the side signal (9) from the back signal (12), for an output signal strength 3. Enough strength to set off that TNT.

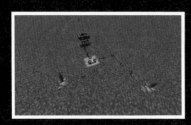

Comparators can also measure containers and produce a signal whose strength depends on how full the container is. You can read more about this in chapter 1. No signal is produced when the container is empty, and a full strength signal is produced when the container is completely full. Comparators can also measure a cake (how many slices it has), item frames (what position the item is rotated to), and cauldrons (how much water they have).

The cake on the left is whole with its full 7 slices intact. Each slice has a value of 2 (for cake fullness sensing). Its comparator sends out the maximum uneaten cake power strength of 14. The cake on the right has a slice taken from it. So its comparator sends out a cake power signal that is only 12 blocks strong.

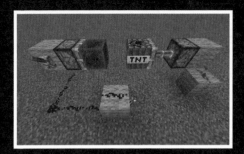

edstone devices are objects that do something when you give them a redstone signal. Dispensers and droppers eject items, trapdoors open, and pistons extend their arms.

Dispensers

Dispensers and droppers look like they have faces. The dispenser looks surprised!

When you power a dispenser, it ejects one item, chosen randomly from its inventory. It has a 9-slot inventory that you access by right-clicking it.

Dispenser recipe.

The dispenser ejects most items in the same way you drop items with the Q key (or another key assigned to the Drop Item command). It drops items into the one block in front of it. However, with some items, it will place and/or activate the item. These special interactions include:

- Armor—Puts armor and shields on a player if the player is within 1 block and has that armor slot empty

- Boats—Places boats in water

- Bonemeal—Applies bonemeal to a crop

- Bucket—Removes a lava or water source

- Fire Charge—Explode with fireballs toward a target

- Fireworks—Places and activates fireworks

- Flint and steel—Sets fire to the block in front

- Lava bucket—Places a lava source

- Minecarts—Places minecarts on a rail (if rail is there)

- Mob Heads—Places pumpkins or mob heads on players, mobs and stands. Completes golems and withers when the appropriate head is dispensed

- Projectiles—Throws or fires a projectile (these include arrows, eggs, snowballs, and splash potions)

- Shulker Boxes—places shulker boxes

- TNT—Places and activates TNT

- Water bucket—Places a water source

When a dispenser ejects any item other than a projectile, it clicks and releases smoke particles. When you place a dispenser, it will always face toward you. If you need it to face a particular direction, first stand in that direction.

Doors

These include all types of doors, fence gates, and trapdoors. Doors open when you give them a redstone signal and close when the signal stops.

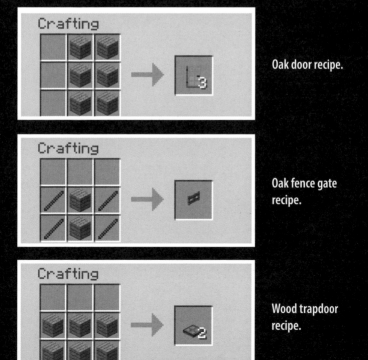

Oak door recipe.

Oak fence gate recipe.

Wood trapdoor recipe.

Iron trapdoor recipe.

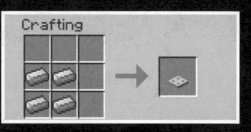

Droppers

A dropper is almost identical to a dispenser. It has a 9-slot inventory and it ejects items through its front, just like a dispenser. There are two main differences. First, the dropper never activates, places, or fires items. Second, it can place items in containers placed in front of it. When you power a dropper, it ejects 1 item chosen randomly from its inventory. Droppers can also eject items through a block of glass.

A dropper looks the same as a dispenser except for its smile!

Dropper recipe.

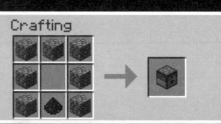

A hopper moves items around from one inventory to another. It will suck in any items that you drop into the one block of air above it. A hopper will also automatically take items from a chest or container placed directly above it. It transfers items to any container that its output tube (at the bottom) points to.

Hoppers transfer items to other containers.

Hoppers can remove and add items to: chests, furnaces, dispensers, droppers, brewing stands, other hoppers, and minecarts with chests and hoppers. Unlike many redstone devices, if a hopper *receives* redstone power, it will stop transferring items. A hopper has an inventory with only 5 slots.

Hopper recipe.

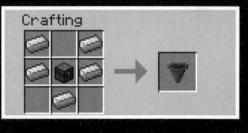

You will need to press shift when you right-click to place a hopper on top of some objects, like chests. If you want a hopper to point to a chest or another item sideways (rather than from above), shift-right-click the side of the chest or item with the hopper in your hand.

Shift-right-click on a chest or container with the hopper to make the hopper's output tube point to that chest.

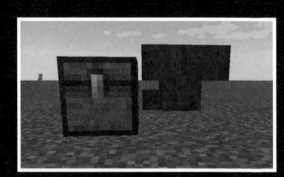

More about Hoppers:

- Hoppers transfer items one at a time, starting with the leftmost slot in an inventory.

- You can make a hopper pipe of several hoppers in a chain, one pointing to the next.

- Hoppers can only work with chests that can be opened. If your cat is sitting on a chest, the hopper won't pull or push items to it. Also, hoppers don't work with Ender chests.

- When a hopper is above a brewing stand, it only transfers items to the stand's top ingredient slot. When it is pointed to the side of the stand, it only transfers to the potion slots. When it is below the stand, it only takes from the potion slots.

- When a hopper is above a furnace, it transfers items only to the ingredient slot. When it points to the furnace side, it only transfers fuel items. When it is beneath the furnace, it only takes smelted items.

Minecart Rails

Two types of minecart rails are devices. If you power an activator rail, it will activate certain types of minecarts that run over it. Regular minecarts will eject any mobs or players in them. Hopper minecarts will *stop* picking up items. TNT minecarts will set off the TNT.

Detector rail recipe.

Powered rails respond to a redstone signal by speeding up a minecart passing over them. They're used to keep minecarts going fast and to propel them uphill.

Powered rail recipe.

Note Blocks

When you send a note block a power signal, it plays a musical note—F sharp. You can right-click a note block repeatedly to make the note a half-note higher. After 24 clicks (two octaves) it changes back to the original F# note. Note blocks need a block of air above them in order to make their sound. The tone of a note block depends on what kind of surface they are on. On many blocks, like dirt, they make the sound of a piano. On wood they sound like a guitar, and on some other blocks, a drum.

Note block recipe.

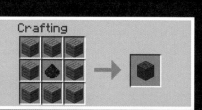

When you power a piston or a sticky piston block, it uses a wooden arm to extend its front side, called its head, out one block. Any block that was in front of it is pushed as well. When the power signal is removed, the piston retracts. With a regular piston, the block it pushed remains where it is. With a sticky piston, the block it pushed retreats with the head.

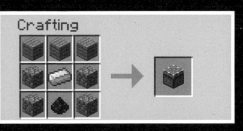

Piston recipe.

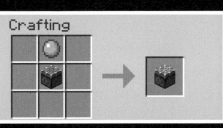

Sticky piston recipe.

Either type of piston can move up to 12 blocks in front of it. However, when a sticky piston retracts, it only pulls back the one block it touches. The regular piston pulls back no blocks.

When you place a piston, its head faces toward you. To get it to face a particular direction, you need to move to the location you want it to face.

There are some blocks a piston can't move. These include bedrock, obsidian, portal blocks, and anvils. Pistons also cannot move blocks that can perform special actions. These include beds, brewing stands, chests, dispensers, droppers, hoppers, furnaces, and chests. Also, some blocks will turn into their drops when a piston pushes them: These include cacti, doors, dragon eggs, flowers, melons, pumpkins, sugar cane, and torches.

Slime blocks react in a special way with pistons. You can push *and* pull up to 12 total connected slime blocks (and regular blocks that are connected to a slime block). All these blocks *don't* have to be directly in front of the piston's head. A sticky piston will also move regular blocks not connected directly to a slime block as long as the total blocks to move add up to 12 or less. It won't pull these back, however.

A sticky piston can move blocks that aren't directly in front of it, as long as they are connected by slime (and don't number more than 12).

Redstone Lamps

A redstone lamp is like a glowstone lamp and is made with glowstone. It will only turn on when it gets a redstone power signal. They are often used to make street lighting (hooked up with an inverted daylight sensor) as well as home and mob trap lighting.

Redstone lamp recipe.

TNT

There are several ways to set off TNT. It will go off if it's touched by fire or lava or the explosion of another TNT. You can ignite TNT with a flint and steel or shoot it with a fire charge or a bow enchanted with Flame I. You can also set it off with redstone. A redstone signal will activate it, and a dispenser can place and activate TNT in its inventory.

TNT recipe.

CHAPTER 4

AUTO SMELTER

This small automatic smelter is very easy to make and quite helpful in a survival world. Drop smeltable items and fuel in the top two chests, and they'll all end up smelted in the bottom.

What You Need:

3 chests

3 hoppers

1 furnace

*I've also used additional blocks—red brick, red brick stairs, and stone bricks—to decorate this build.

1. Dig a hole one wide and 2 long. At the front of the hole, place your chest.

2. In the hole behind the chest, place a hopper that is pointing toward the chest. (To do so, press shift and right-click the back of the chest while you hold the hopper.)

3. Place a furnace on top of the hopper. (To do this, shift-right-click the hopper with the furnace in your hand.)

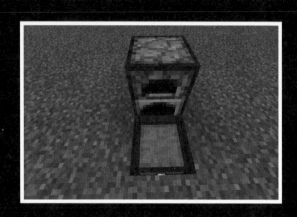

4. Place a hopper pointing into the side of the chest, and another above the chest. The side hopper will place coal or other fuel into the fuel slot, and the upper hopper will place smeltable items into the furnace's top slot.

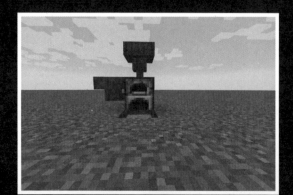

5. Place two chests, one above each hopper you placed in step 4. The hoppers below will automatically remove items from the chest above them. You are done! You can pretty the contraption up, as I did below, or just start using it. You can also easily modify this to use double chests. And since there's no redstone dust or repeaters and such, an accidental water spill won't destroy this contraption.

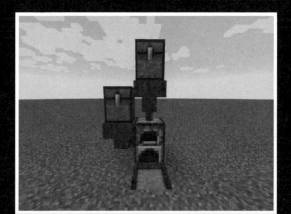

CHAPTER 5

TNT CANNON

What's more fun than blowing stuff up with TNT? Blowing stuff up with a TNT cannon! This is a classic Minecraft cannon, with some extra blocks to make it look a bit more like an actual old-timey weapon.

WARNING

When you are working with TNT and redstone, always wait till the very end before you place the TNT. It is very easy to set off TNT accidentally when you are playing around with redstone connected to it!

What You Need:

26 spruce wood planks

8 (4x2) spruce wood steps

2 spruce wood fences

3 stone blocks

1 stone button

56 coal blocks

18 redstone dust

4 repeaters

7 TNT (for each cannon shot!)

1 bucket of water

1. Build your cannon's base, or carriage, out of 18 spruce wood planks. First, place two rows of 3 planks. On top of this bottom level, place three rows of 3 planks. This level should be offset from the bottom level by 1 block. Above the middle row of this level, build just one row of 3 planks.

2. Add the bottom of the cannon. Make a 3-block wide and 9-block long rectangle of coal blocks.

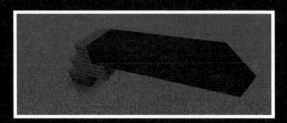

3. Add the sides, front, and back of the cannon. Add a 1-block coal block row to the two sides of the cannon, and 1 block at either end, between the two long rows.

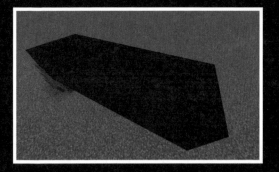

4. Add the axle for the wheels. Underneath the cannon, next to the spruce wood base, place one row, 3 blocks long, of stone blocks.

5. Increase the size of the cannon's base. Add a 2-block wide, 3-block long row of coal blocks next to the axle, to make the cannon's base, or breech, look a little bigger than the muzzle of the cannon.

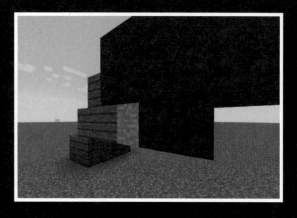

6. On each end of the axle, build out large wheels for the carriage. First, build a cross shape, with a space in the center, of spruce wood blocks.

7. Add spruce wood stairs to round out the wheels. Add a spruce wood fence in the center of each wheel.

8. At the back, or breech, of the cannon, place 1 coal block, 1 block in from the sides and 1 block above.

9. Right underneath the block you placed in step 8, use your water bucket to place a water source block. The water should run 8 blocks, from here just to the front of the cannon.

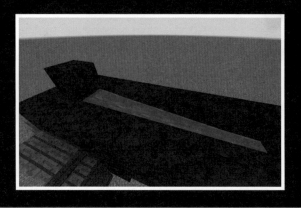

10. On one side of the cannon, place 8 redstone dust in a line, starting from the backmost block. At the cannon's muzzle, there should be 1 block without redstone.

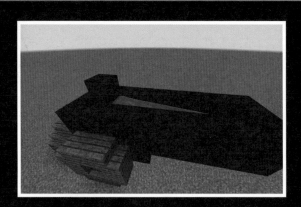

11. On the other side of the cannon, starting from the back-most block, place a line of 2 redstone dust, followed by 4 repeaters that point toward the muzzle. Right-click each of the repeaters 3 times to give them each the maximum 4-tick delay.

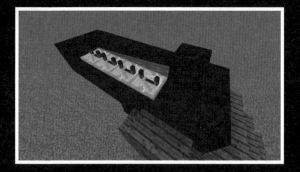

12. We're now going to continue this side's redstone signal with redstone dust, but also raise it up 1 block. This way the signal can reach the TNT that we'll be placing in the muzzle. Add 2 coal blocks to the very end of the side we are working on. Use 3 redstone dust to run the signal from the repeaters to the muzzle.

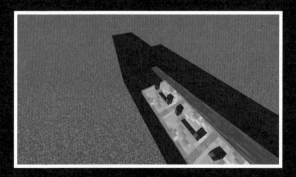

13. Place 1 redstone dust at the back of the cannon to join the two sides of dust. Place another 4 redstone dust to bring the redstone signal down to one side of the carriage.

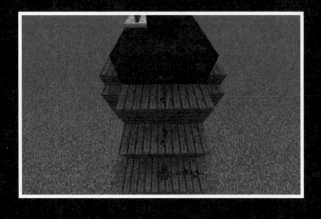

14. On the same side of the carriage, place the button you'll use to set the cannon off.

15. Place 1 block of TNT at the very end of the cannon at the muzzle, on top of the last coal block. This is the TNT that will be burst from the cannon.

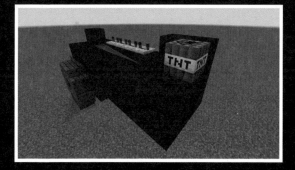

16. Place 6 TNT in the center water channel. (The water will look like it's disappearing; that is fine.) Be careful not to place TNT under the raised block at the back of the cannon, where you placed the water source. If you do, the water will disappear, and you'll need to replace it. The raised block is there to help remind you!

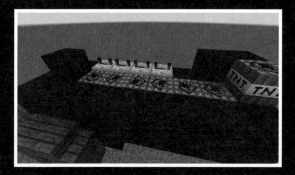

17. Press the button and stand back!! Enjoy watching the first 6 TNT build up power to blast the last one off before it explodes itself.

How Does It Work?

When you press the button, the redstone signal is carried on one side of the cannon to all six of the TNT in the water channel. The water will prevent the TNT from causing damage to any blocks, but it will set off and propel the TNT on the very end. On the other side of the cannon, the signal travels to the seventh TNT. It is delayed by the repeaters so that it doesn't explode before the six TNT in the water. It will explode after it has been hurled from the cannon. Sometimes it may go a little farther than other times, and sometimes it can explode in the air.

CHAPTER 6

SUPERFAST MINI FARM

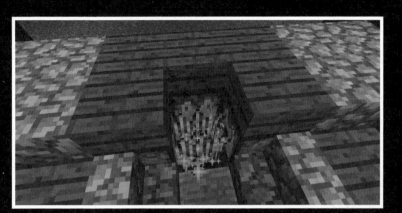

his is the smallest farm you can have—it's only one block of
dirt! But it can get you a stack of wheat, carrots, or potatoes
in a hurry, if you have the bonemeal. In fact, because it relies on
bonemeal, you may want to place this near your skeleton farm!

What You Need:

1 sticky piston

3 dispensers

3 repeaters

1 stone pressure plate

2 redstone torches

11 redstone dust

1 bucket of water

Lots of bonemeal

2–3 crop starters (grass seeds, carrots, or potatoes)

2+ building blocks (I've used 1 light blue wool and 1 orange wool in the contraption. For the décor I've used cobble, stone brick, spruce wood planks, slabs of these three, plus spruce wood, glowstone, and cobble stairs.)

1. Dig a 1x1 hole 3 blocks deep. At the bottom, place a sticky piston facing up. On top of the sticky piston, place a block of dirt. This will be the single block of dirt you farm on! (The piston will extend later on to make the dirt flush with the ground.)

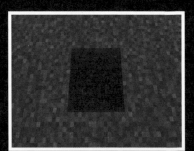

2. Replace the block of dirt in front of the hole with a block of your choice (I've used light blue wool), and on top of that place a stone pressure plate. This will be what you stand on when you are farming. The pressure plate will activate the contraption.

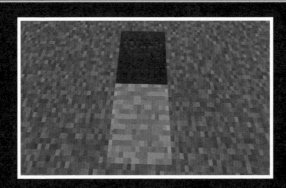

3. Around the other three sides of the hole, place dispensers facing inward. These will place three bonemeal on your farm to make your crops grow really fast.

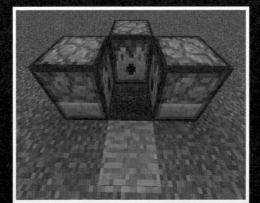

4. Dig out the sides and front around the light blue wool, in a U-shape. This trench should be 2 blocks deep. Also dig out the 1 block of dirt beneath the light blue wool.

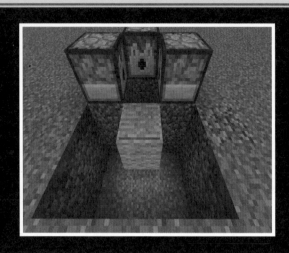

5. At the bottom of the trench, and to the right of the light blue wool, place another block. I've used orange wool here.

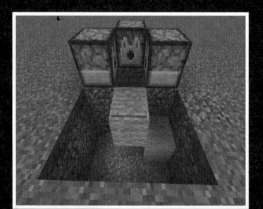

6. Now we're going to make a timing mechanism, or clock, that we'll use later to move our single block of dirt up and down. First, place a repeater pointing to the orange wool. Place a redstone torch on the front side of the orange wool.

7. Connect the redstone torch to the back of the repeater with 3 redstone dust. The clock should start flashing on and off! Your clock should also sizzle out after a few rounds. This is called burn out and it happens to torches when the timing is too fast for them to keep up. To slow the pulse down, right-click the repeater once to give it a 2-tick delay. After a few moments, the torch will relight and the clock will start up again.

8. Now we are going to connect the clock to the pressure plate above. Place a redstone torch on the front of the light blue wool. This powers the redstone trail below it, turning off the torch on the orange wool. Now, when you step on the pressure plate, the torch beneath it will turn off. This will let the clock start pulsing again.

9. Next connect the clock to the sticky piston. Dig out the block that is two blocks beneath the left dispenser and place one redstone dust there. This powers on the piston, which extends and pushes the dirt block up.

10. Now we can connect the clock to the dispensers. On the center and right dispensers, place 2 repeaters pointing into them as shown. The repeaters help the redstone dust point in the right direction at the dispensers.

11. Dig out a trench, on the right of the contraption, to carry the redstone trail up from the clock to the two repeaters you have just placed. You'll need 6 redstone dust for this trail.

12. The third dispenser can be connected by placing 1 redstone dust to its side.

13. Now dig a hole behind the left dispenser and place your water in it. This will help keep the farm hydrated.

14. We're ready to test the farm. Add lots of bonemeal to the three dispensers, and hoe the dirt block between them so that it is ready for planting. To get your farm to start, stand on the pressure plate. With your wheat seeds (or carrots or potatoes) in your hand, right-click (and keep the right-click pressed) on the soil as it moves up and down. The dispensers will dispense bonemeal quickly. (The dispensers only place bonemeal if there is a crop before them.) As soon as your crop is mature it will pop off the dirt and into you!

NOTE: The pressure plate only gives out a signal when you are standing on it. If you replace it with a lever, you can turn your mechanism on and off so you can walk around it. Of course, it won't be planting or bonemealing crops, but you can look around to see the redstone flashing and the piston moving.

15. Now you can add any design touches you want. Here, I've covered up the redstone with cobble, stone brick, and spruce wood, and added spruce and glowstone columns.

I also added stairs up to the platform and down to the farming pressure plate. It might be a good idea to also add chests to hold bonemeal, hoes, seeds, and crops.

NOTE: When you decorate around your contraptions, be careful to leave space above the redstone dust. When redstone is being trailed up a block in a staircase fashion, the vertical trail going up (on the side of the block) also needs a block of space above it. It is easy to forget and cover this up, and stop the redstone pulse from traveling.

CHAPTER 1

COMBINATION LOCK

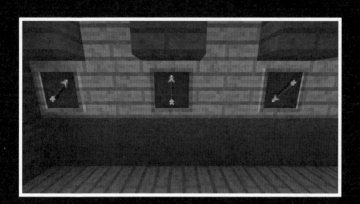

This combination lock on your door will keep strangers away from your precious goods! It uses three numbers, but you can easily expand it to use four, five, or more numbers, as you will see. This lock is best for an area that you will only open temporarily while you are there, like a special storage area.

The lock is based on the way that comparators behave with item frames. You've probably already seen that an item in an item frame can be rotated and goes through eight positions. A comparator can produce a signal based on that position. The item frame must be placed on a block behind the comparator for this to work. When there is no item in the frame, the comparator produces no signal. When you place an item in, and the item is straight up and down (or, the same way its icon appears in the Minecraft inventory), the comparator makes a signal strength of 1. Each time the item is rotated, the comparator increases the signal strength by one, up to the last position before it returns to normal, 8.

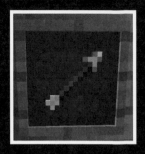

The arrow in this item frame is in the same position as the arrow icon you see in your inventory. Because it is in the default position, an attached comparator will send the default signal strength of 1.

Before creating your combination lock, decide what your three-number combination number will be. Each number must be between 1 and 8. The number of blocks and redstone you use will depend on your combination, as you will see. For this tutorial, we're using the combination number 3-8-5. Once you work through this project, you will see how you can easily change it to use your own secret number.

What You Need:

64+ blocks of your choice (I've used 33 birch blocks, 3 lime green wool, 27 yellow wool, and 1 magenta wool.)

1 iron door

3 item frames

3 arrows

3 comparators

4 redstone torches

4 repeaters

60+ redstone dust

1. Build a wall that is 3 blocks high and 11 blocks long using blocks of your choice. (I've used birch wood blocks.) Leave a 2-block space for a door on the right, 1 block in from the right side. This is the wall your lock and door will be on.

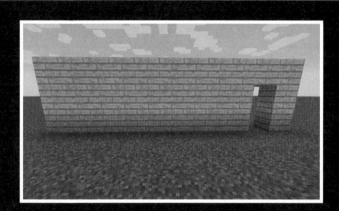

2. Place the iron door in the space you've left, and place 3 item frames 1 block up from the bottom of the wall, and spaced 1 block apart from each other, as shown. There should be 3 blocks between the rightmost item frame and the door. (The recipe for an item frame is 1 leather surrounded by 8 sticks.)

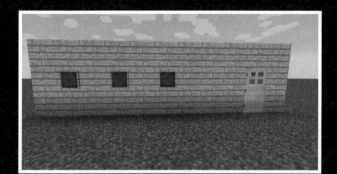

3. In each item frame, place an arrow. It should be pointing diagonally to the upper left, just as the arrow in your Minecraft inventory looks. This is position 1.

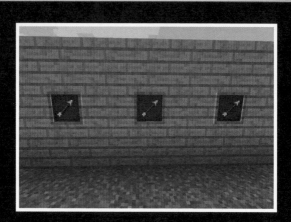

NOTE: For the item frame, you can choose any item that will clearly show what position it is in. This will be any item that isn't vertically symmetrical. Its top and bottom should be different, like an arrow, a sword, or a feather. If you use something that looks very much the same when it is rotated, like a snowball, it will be difficult to tell what position it is in.

4. Rotate each arrow to the position that shows what number it is. We are using the numbers 3 – 8 – 5 for the lock, so click the leftmost item frame 2 times to move the arrow to the 3 position. Click the middle item frame 7 times, and click the right frame 4 times.

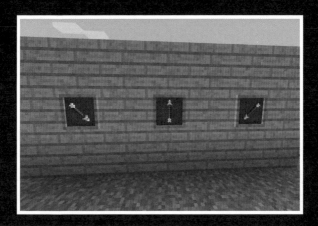

5. Behind the wall, place 3 blocks on the ground, exactly opposite the item frames. I've used lime green wool. On top of these, place 3 comparators facing away from the item frames. Because the comparators are already detecting the item frames, they will light up.

6. Now let's test the signal strength of each comparator. Just above and in front of each comparator, place a row of 9 blocks (I've used yellow wool), for a total of 3 rows. On top of each of

these yellow wool blocks place redstone dust. Now look at how far the redstone signal travels on each. The comparator behind the leftmost item frame at position 3 should have 3 blocks of dust lit up. The second comparator should send the signal 8 blocks, and the third or rightmost should send the signal only 5 blocks. (If you have different results, check the position of the item in the item frame.)

7. Now remove all of the blocks on these rows that are not carrying signal, leaving just the redstone and yellow wool blocks that are lit up. The left row will be 3 blocks long, the middle will be 8 blocks long, and the right will be 5 blocks long.

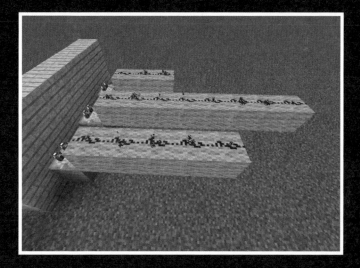

8. On the very end of all 3 rows, place a redstone torch as shown. Notice that the signal traveling from the comparator turns these torches off.

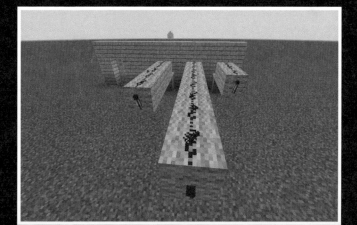

9. Beneath each row, add redstone dust that reaches from the green wool holding the comparator to the block right below the torch at the end.

10. At the end of each line of redstone you just placed, add a repeater facing away from the wall.

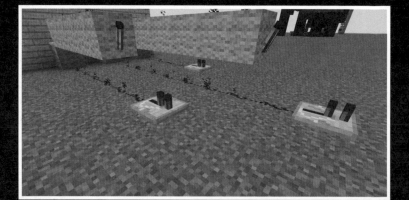

11. At the end of the longest row of yellow blocks add 1 red-stone dust. Add enough redstone dust at the end of the other 2 rows so that they reach the same length as the first, as shown.

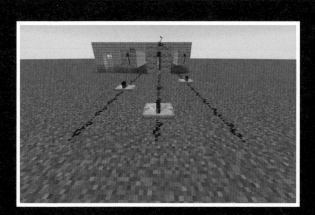

12. Use 2 redstone dust to connect the 3 lines at their ends.

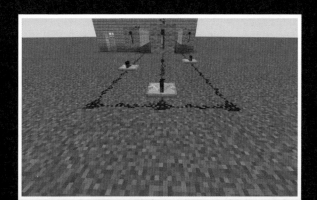

13. At the end of the redstone line nearest the door, place 3 redstone dust to bring the signal out and then change direction toward the door, as shown.

14. Place a repeater facing toward the door at the end of the line you just created.

15. Run redstone dust from the repeater all the way back to the wall. Stop just 1 block before you reach the wall.

16. At the wall, on the same side as your redstone, break the 2 blocks next to the door and the 2 blocks in front of this, as shown.

17. Now use 3 redstone dust to connect the trail to the block beside the door, as shown.

18. At the moment, the redstone is working the *opposite* to the way we want it. The door will remain closed whenever the combination is right. It will open whenever the combination is wrong. Test this out by changing the position of an arrow in one of the item frames. To fix this, we change the signal to be the opposite of what it is now. First, break 2 of the redstone dust in the last trail that leads to the door.

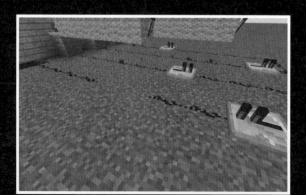

19. On the side closest to the last repeater, place 1 block. I've used magenta wool.

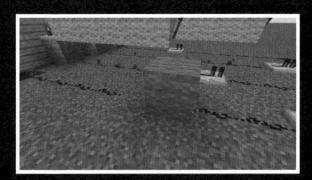

20. On the front side of the block you just placed, facing the wall, place a redstone torch. The redstone torch will be turned off from any signal coming to the block it is on. If there is no signal, it will send its own signal to the door. Congratulations! You are done with the redstone! Go test your lock, changing the item frames to the right positions and the wrong positions.

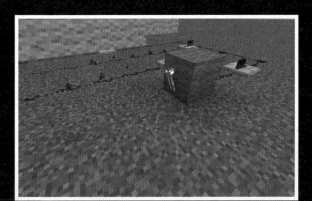

21. Now you can add any design touches you want. Here, I've created a storage building. I closed off the redstone section and added a storage room with lots of chests, furnaces, and crafting tables. I've used jungle wood, acacia and birch wood planks, slabs, and stairs, orange-stained clay, glowstone, and birch wood fence.

How to Customize the Lock

You can change this lock so that it uses your own private number. You will need to change the length of each row of redstone behind the item frame to match the numbers you choose. To do this, just follow steps 4 through 12 again to determine how long the row needs to be and to hook it up to the rest of the rows. You can also add more numbers, by copying and adding the same pattern of item frame, comparator, redstone dust, and repeaters to this setup.

How It Works

Each item frame–comparator combination sends out a signal whose length in blocks is the same as the item's position. If the item frame arrow is in the wrong position, the comparator will send out a signal that is either too long or too short. If the signal is too long, the redstone dust beneath the yellow wool will reach the repeater, and turn the redstone signal to the final repeater on. (The final repeater is there to make sure none of the redstone signals fizzle out because the lines of dust are too long.) If the signal is too short, the redstone dust will not reach either the top torch or the bottom repeater. However, this lets the redstone torch turn back on. The torch then powers the redstone signal reaching the final repeater before the door. If any signal comes through to the final repeater, the repeater will send along the signal to the torch and turn off. The torch off means that no signal to open the door will reach the door. Only when *all* of the three possible signals from the comparators are *off* will a redstone signal, from the very last redstone torch, reach the door and open it.

CHAPTER 8

AUTOMATIC STORAGE SYSTEM

nce you've been mining for a while in Minecraft, you start getting lots of stuff. Lots of coal, lots of redstone, lapis, gold, iron, and hopefully diamonds! You can use a redstone contraption to help sort all your loot out when you make it back home. This sorting and storage system will let you put everything into a single chest. Then it will sort all these items and place them into separate chests for you! Best of all, you can easily expand it later with more chests to hold more stuff.

What You Need:

8 single chests

6 single trapped chests

39 blocks of your choice (I've used 12 birch wood planks, 3 red wool, 6 light blue wool, 6 lime green wool, 6 white wool, and 6 yellow wool.) On the finished contraption, I've used additional blocks for decoration (birch wood stairs, planks, and slabs and spruce wood).

6 comparators

6 repeaters

37 hoppers

12 redstone dust

6 redstone torches

6 item frames (or, to make these, 48 sticks and 6 leather)

12 samples of storage items (For each type of item you want to store, you will need 2 blocks or pieces of that item, 1 for the item frame and 1 for a hopper that helps sort items. For this example system, you'll need 2 diamonds, 2 gold ingots, 2 iron ingots, 2 coal ore, 2 lapis ore, and 2 redstone dust.)

126 buffer items to use in the filtering system (You will need to choose an item that you don't want to store in your system AND that can stack to 64. I've used 126 dandelions, but you could use 126 jungle saplings or 126 cobble, for example.)

1. Create a 2-block wide by 6-block long platform for your chests. One long side will be the front of your storage system.

2. Place 2 single chests at one end of the platform to create 1 double chest.

3. In front of the double chest, place 2 trapped chests to make a double trapped chest. Trapped chests are like regular chests, except they produce a redstone signal when they are opened. But they have another handy trait that we are using them for. They can be placed right up against a regular chest. This means you can alternate placing regular chests and trapped chests to fit more chests in the same area.

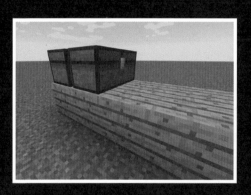

4. Alternate placing double chests and trapped double chests on your base, until you have 6 double chests total on your base.

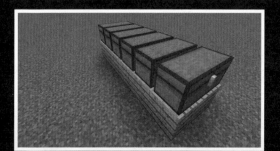

5. On the front of the platform, place an item frame below each chest. Right-click each item frame with the item you want to place in that chest. I've put in diamond, gold ingot, iron ingot, redstone, lapis lazuli, and coal. (You can craft an item frame with 1 leather surrounded by 8 sticks.)

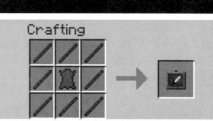

Item frame recipe.

6. On the other side of the chests—the back side of the platform—place a row of 6 blocks (I've used lime green wool) 1 block away from the platform.

7. On the far side of each lime green wool, place a repeater facing into the wool.

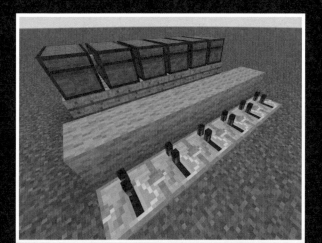

8. On the other side of each lime green wool, place a redstone torch.

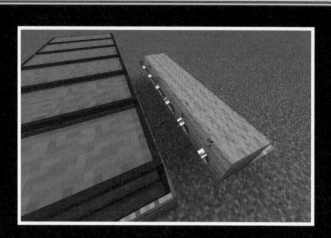

9. On top of the redstone torches, place a row of 6 hoppers. Each hopper should face into the chest next to it. You can make it do this by pressing shift as you right-click with the hopper.

10. Place a row of 6 blocks (I've used light blue wool) next to this bottom row of hoppers and above the row of lime green wool.

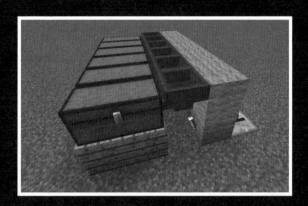

11. On top of the light blue wool, place a row of 6 comparators. Each comparator should be facing away from the chests and hoppers.

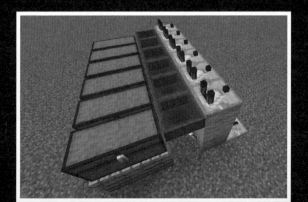

12. Above the bottom row of hoppers, place another row of 6 hoppers. Each hopper should point into the comparators. To do this, press shift as you right-click the back side of each comparator.

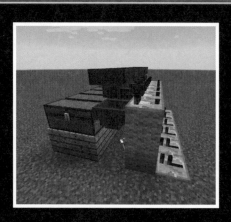

13. On the other side of the comparators, place a row of 6 blocks of your choice alongside the light blue wool. I've used yellow wool here. On top of each block, place 1 redstone dust.

14. On the back side of the row of repeaters on the ground, place a row of 6 blocks of your choice. I've used white wool. On top of each block, place 1 redstone dust. (This will connect to the redstone on the yellow wool.)

15. In this storage system, items are placed in a chest on the left to be sorted into the 6 chests, and any items that overflow or don't match one of the 6 stored items will be collected by a chest on the right. Make a base for the overflow chest by placing a column of 3 blocks of your choice (I've used red wool) at the far right, to the right of the last redstone torch. On top, place 1 chest.

16. Above the second row of hoppers, place another row of 7 hoppers. The first hopper you place should point into the overflow chest. Each of the next hoppers should point into the last hopper you placed. The seventh and final hopper you place will collect items from your input chest.

17. Place a chest above the last hopper you placed in step 16. This will be the input chest. Anything you put in this leftmost chest will travel down the line of top hoppers. It will be sorted into the chests below if it matches or end up in the overflow chest if it doesn't.

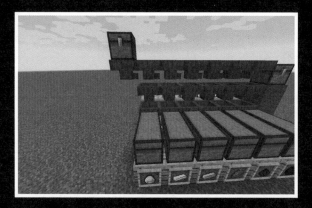

18. Now we need to configure the filtering system. The middle row of hoppers is used to filter and sort items. Each hopper will sort items for the chest it is next to. Right-click the hopper for the first chest. There are 5 inventory slots. Into the left inventory slot, place just 1 item of the type the chest is storing. I've put in 1 diamond, as this is my diamond chest. In the next 4 slots, place 21 items of your 126 buffer items. My buffer item is dandelions. I've put 1 dandelion in slots 2, 3, and 4, and 18 in slot 5, total 21 buffer items. It doesn't matter which slot they go into, as long as there are items in all of the four slots and they total 21.

19. Repeat this for the other 5 chests. Into the middle hopper for each chest, place 1 item of what the chest stores (the item you placed in the chest's item frame), plus 21 buffer items. Here are the hopper inventories from all six chests that store diamonds, gold ingots, iron ingots, lapis lazuli ore, redstone dust, and coal ore.

20. The contraption is finished! You can test the system by adding blocks to the input chest on the left. (The first time you run this, 1 item of each storage type will remain in the bottom hopper for its matching chest. This is fine, leave it in the bottom hopper.)

Blocks that don't match anything will move to the overflow chest. If blocks aren't ending up at the right chest, go over each construction step. Make sure the hoppers, comparators, and repeaters are pointing in the right direction, and that your buffer item isn't one of the ones you are storing.

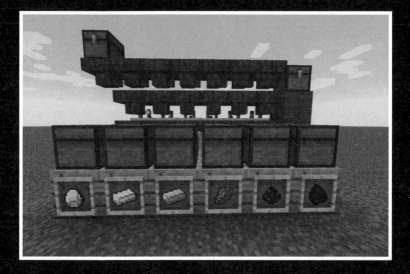

21. Finally, add any finishing design touches you want to cover the redstone up and make it easy to access all your chests. I've used birch wood planks, slabs, and stairs, and spruce wood to decorate this system.

Expanding Your Storage

Expanding your storage is very easy. For each chest you want to add, you will add 1 double chest (or trapped chest) and the blocks that go with it at the end of the line of chests and before the overflow chest. You'll need 1 item frame, 1 repeater, 1 comparator, 3 hoppers, 2 redstone dust, 1 redstone torch, and the blocks to hold these on, for each new chest. Don't forget to add the filter materials for each chest's middle hopper: 21 buffer items and 1 of the item the chest will hold.

How It Works

An item you drop in the input chest travels down the top row of hoppers, in the direction the hoppers face. At each hopper, it checks below to see if it can fit into that hopper's inventory. Let's say the item is coal. At the diamond chest, it will see the middle hopper. This hopper's inventory slots all have either diamonds or the buffer item, dandelions. So nothing but diamonds or dandelions will fit into this hopper. The coal ore moves along until it reaches the hopper with 1 coal and 21 dandelions. Here it can fit! So the coal drops down into the middle hopper.

There are 23 items in this hopper now, and the hopper gives out a slightly stronger signal to the comparator it is facing. The output signal resulting from 22 items reached the 1 redstone dust in front of the comparator, while the signal from 23 items can reach the second redstone dust (1 block down). Now the signal can reach the repeater below, and turn the redstone torch off. This redstone torch was locking the very bottom hopper. With the redstone torch turned off now, the coal ore can pass through. Once the middle hopper has only 22 items again, it stops sending the signal that keeps the torch off, and the hopper stops sending items through to the chest.

CHAPTER 9

MOB CRUSHER

The great thing about XP mob farms is that they let you kill mobs safely and in one spot, so you can gather all the XP and items they drop. It is helpful to "soften" the mobs up first by damaging them so that they only have one heart left. That way, you can just punch them once to get the XP—and you don't have to use up the durability of your weapons.

In this crusher, you'll use pistons to crush mobs, suffocating them to damage them, in a tiny 1x1 room. How you get the mobs there is up to you! One easy way is to use a water channel to push the mobs from a mob spawning room. (If you are not sure how to make a mob spawning room, see the notes at the end of this project!) This crusher will deal enough damage to mobs so that you can kill them afterwards with one hit.

What You Need:

2 sticky pistons

30 blocks of your choice (I've used colored wool to help show the steps, stone bricks, and glass.)

1 stone button

8 redstone dust

2 comparators

1 repeater

2 hoppers

3 redstone torches

*This doesn't include any blocks you use to gather and move your mobs into the grinder.

1. Plan your location. You will want to place the crushing room somewhere that you will have mobs you can push into it. Here I have a water channel that drops mobs down 2 blocks at the end, where the crushing room will be.

2. Place 2 sticky pistons at the back of what will be the crushing room, one on top of the other. Leave a 1-block space in front of each for the blocks the pistons will push.

3. Add the 2 blocks you will be using to crush the mob, placing them against the pistons' fronts. These 2 blocks are the back wall of the room. I've used purple wool.

4. Catty-corner to the bottom purple wool, place 2 blocks of your choice. I've used yellow wool.

5. On top of the yellow wool, place 2 hoppers pointing at each other. To do this, you place 1 hopper first on the yellow wool. Then place a second hopper, pointing to the first, by shift-clicking the side of the first hopper. You will now need to break the first hopper. Replace it so that it points at the second hopper by shift-clicking the second hopper's side. The 2 hoppers' bottom funnels should point right at each other as shown in the picture.

6. Behind the yellow wool and hoppers, place 2 blocks of your choice. (I've used lime green wool.) On top of these place 2 comparators pointing away from the hoppers. The arrows on the comparators should face the back of the contraption.

7. Next to the bottom piston, place 1 redstone dust.

8. Above the dust you just placed, and next to the top piston, place 2 blocks of your choice side by side. I've used cyan wool.

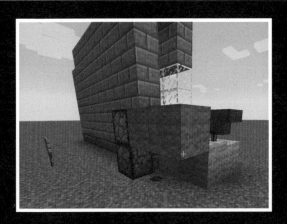

9. Place a redstone torch on the cyan wool that is farthest from the crushing room.

10. Next to the green wool and comparators, place another building block. (I've used orange wool.) On top of this, place a repeater that is facing the front of the contraption. The arrow should be pointing in the opposite direction as the comparators' arrows.

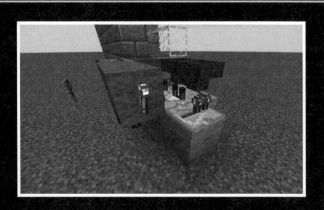

11. Place a block next to the outside hopper. I've used pink wool here. On top of this, place 1 redstone dust.

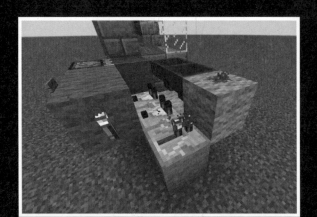

12. Now, on top of the outside hopper, place 3 blocks in an upside-down L shape. I've used light blue wool in the picture.

13. On the side of the top left block of light blue wool, place a redstone torch. Along the top place 2 redstone dust.

14. Now on the inside of the upside-down L, place 1 redstone torch.

15. Now you will place the blocks and redstone dust that will connect to the button you use to turn the crusher on. Here I've used 4 red wool with 4 redstone dust on top of each. The last wool block has a stone button to use for starting the contraption.

16. The hoppers you placed in step 5 are a type of timer. To make this work, place 12 blocks or items of your choice (I've used cobble) in the left, or outer, hopper. To do this, you can right-click the hopper to open its inventory, and drag the 12 blocks from your own inventory.

17. Congratulations! Except for finishing the crushing room, the contraption is done. Test it by pressing the button. The 2 pistons should extend for about 15 seconds, then retract. If they don't retract, go through all of the previous steps to make sure every item is placed correctly or pointing the right way.

18. Now all you have to do is finish the crushing room. The room will be just the 1x1 block of space that is at least 2 blocks high. If you are pushing or dropping your mobs in, it may need to be higher. The room I have is 4 blocks high so that mobs can come in from the water channel with a 2-block drop. Add blocks of your choice above the purple wool at the back wall. Add blocks to finish off the ceiling and left wall. I've used stone bricks and glass.

19. For the front wall of the crushing room use 2 half-slabs (placed as the top halves of blocks) as shown. This gives you space to swat at the crushed mobs. It also prevents any baby zombies from getting out and allows the XP orbs to easily flow to you at the bottom.

The contraption is set up so that the left hopper is powered. Powering a hopper prevents it from sending on items, like the cobblestone placed in it (although it can still receive items). Also notice that the comparator behind the left hopper is lit up, which means that it is receiving a signal from the left hopper. The hopper sends out a redstone signal when it contains items.

When you press the button, the redstone signal turns the left hopper off and the right hopper on. The left hopper starts sending the right hopper the 12 cobble. During this time, you can see that both comparators are lit up, because both hoppers have items. Also, the signal from the right comparator is hooked up to the pistons, so whenever the right comparator has items in it, the pistons are extended.

When the left hopper is empty, it stops sending its signal out through the comparator in the back, and this allows the farthest back torch to turn on. This sends a signal through the repeater. This then turns the front left redstone torch back on, and the front right redstone torch back off. And this powers on the left hopper and powers off the right hopper. The right hopper now sends the 12 items back to the left hopper. Once all 12 items are back to the left hopper, the right hopper's comparator signal turns off and the piston retracts.

More: The 12 items define how long the right comparator is on; it is the full length of time that it takes 12 items to move both to and from the right hopper. It takes 0.7 seconds to transfer 1 item, so transferring 12 items twice (12 x 2 x .7) is 16.8 seconds. If you are using this for mobs with more health than a skeleton, like Endermen or zombies with armor, you can lengthen the crushing time by adding more items to the left hopper. For armored-up zombies, however, you can also try dropping them a few more blocks before entering the crushing room so that they are already a bit damaged.

Mob Spawner Farm

If you have never built a mob XP farm before, the easiest is probably a spawner farm. To collect the mobs that spawn from a dungeon spawner, you first build an 8x8 room, at least 6 blocks high, around a spawner. The spawner should be in the center, in the air. Dig a 2-block deep channel on one side of the room (on the ninth block, so that you still have 8x8 floor space). One block of source water at one end of the channel will push mobs to the other end, where you can dig another 2-block deep hole or channel to keep pushing the mobs with water to where you want them.

In the 8x8 room itself, you need to push the mobs that spawn to the channel. Along the opposite wall from the channel, place water source blocks. Because water travels 8 blocks, this will push mobs right up to the edge of the channel, and they'll drop right in. Here's a picture:

CHAPTER 10

VENDING MACHINE

You will need to choose 1 item as a payment for each item sold (for example, 1 diamond or 1 iron for each chicken, cake, or sword you are going to sell). However, hoppers are always enabled when they have no power going into them, which means that anything we put into the hopper will travel to the bottom chest. Therefore we first must disable the bottom hopper.

What You Need:

2 chests

4 hoppers

Colored wool (1 lime green, 1 blue, 2 magenta, 2 orange, 1 cyan)

3 redstone dust

2 repeaters

3 redstone torches

1 comparator

4 wooden swords

63 items of the payment type (for example, 63 iron ingots)

Stacks of the item you are selling (for example, roast chicken)

Additional building blocks for décor, as you like

1. Dig a hole 5 blocks wide by 4 blocks long that is 3 blocks deep. One of the long sides will be the front, where the vending machine will be.

2. At the bottom of the hole, 1 block in from the left side, place a chest. This is where all the customer payments will end up.

3. Place two hoppers above the chest. Both hoppers should be pointing down.

4. Now dig a two-block-long hole in front of the top hopper.

5. Place two hoppers in this trench. Both should point forward to the hopper in front of it. (In this picture, some of the ground is removed so you can see the correct hopper direction.)

6. Place a chest on top of the front-most hopper. This will be where customers put their payment. Ultimately, the payment will be transferred by the hoppers to the bottom chest.

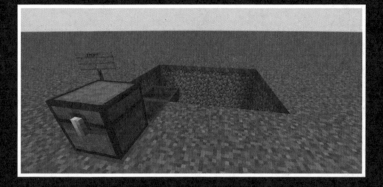

'7. The bottom hopper nearest the bottom chest is where you will place items that decide what kind of payment is needed. However, to work in this contraption, this hopper must be disabled from passing items on. To do this, first place a block (I've used lime green wool) next to the bottom chest, and place 1 redstone dust on top of it. This redstone dust, when it is lit up, will power the hopper, stopping it from passing items along.

8. Place a repeater on the ground, pointing toward the green wool. This repeater will help make sure that the signal going to the bottom hopper doesn't get crossed with other redstone signals in the contraption.

9. One block from the repeater, at the back of the 4x5 hole, place another block (I've used blue wool). On the side of the block that faces the repeater, place a redstone torch. The redstone torch powers the block of space that it is in, so its signal can continue through the repeater and to the redstone dust on the green wool, and to the bottom hopper. Also, because the torch is placed on the side of the wool, it can later be powered off by the signal powering the blue wool.

10. Now we are going to place redstone that will allow the bottom hopper to be powered off very briefly, when payment is made, allowing the payment to drop to the bottom chest. First place 2 blocks (I've used pink wool) behind the chest.

11. On the pink wool nearest the chest, place a comparator pointing away from the chest. This comparator will get a signal from the bottom hopper. The strength of the signal depends on the number of items in the hopper. It reaches full strength when the hopper is full.

12. On the second piece of wool, place a repeater pointing away from the comparator. This repeater helps prevent the signal from the comparator from getting mixed up with other signals in the contraption.

13. Place 2 blocks to the right of the comparator (I've used orange wool). On the top of the block closest to the comparator add 1 redstone dust. On the other, place a redstone torch. This torch is sending a full-strength signal to the comparator. Only when the bottom hopper is full will the hopper's signal to the comparator be equal to the side-signal from the torch. And only then will the comparator produce a signal out its front that will run through the repeater.

14. Now we are going to connect the signal that will come from the comparator to the signal that will turn off the hopper. Behind the block holding the repeater on pink wool, place one redstone dust. If a signal comes from the comparator, this redstone will light up, powering off the redstone torch on the blue wool. The signal to the bottom hopper will be stopped for as long as the comparator is sending out a signal.

15. Now we are going to connect the same signal from the comparator to a circuit that will allow items to be delivered to the customer. Right above the dust you just placed, place another block. I've used cyan wool.

16. On the side of the cyan wool that is above the blue wool, place 1 redstone torch.

17. Above the torch you just placed, place another block (I've used pink wool). On top of this, place another redstone torch. This torch will turn off, because it is receiving a signal from the torch below. When the torch below turns off, it will turn on.

18. Place another block above the redstone torch you placed in step 17. (I've used yellow wool here.)

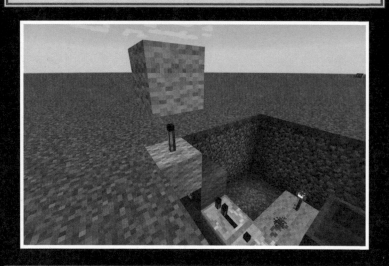

19. Now lay a 3x2 layer of blocks (I've used white wool) as shown.

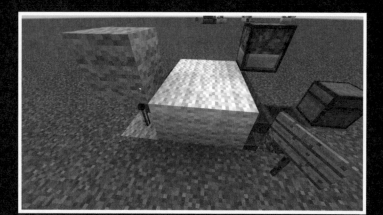

20. On top of the white wool, place 2 blocks (I've used light blue wool) as shown. These white and light blue wool blocks are used to hold a redstone timer that will deliver goods to the customer. In front of the furthest right light-blue wool place a dropper pointing forward.

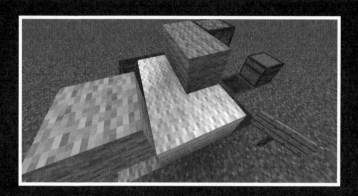

21. Place a comparator pointing toward the front and away from the yellow wool. Right-click it once to set it to "subtract" mode. The front mini-torch on the comparator will light up to show it is in this mode.

22. Place a repeater pointing toward the side of the comparator.

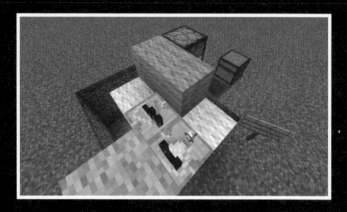

23. Place 4 redstone dust on top of the rest of the white and light blue wool blocks. This creates a circular signal from the comparator, over the light blue wool, to the dropper, to the repeater, and back to the comparator.

24. Almost done! Fill up the dropper with the items you are selling. You can right-click the dropper and drag items from your inventory. (I've used stacks of roasted chicken.)

25. Now, right-click the bottom hopper, above the bottom chest, to open up its inventory. In the leftmost slot, place 63 items of the same type you want for payment. I've used iron ingots, but you could use any stackable item, like emeralds or diamonds. In the four right slots, place 4 wooden swords. Because swords don't stack, they fill up these four slots fully so that they can't be used in the hopper payment transfer. Now the hopper is almost completely full.

26. Your vending machine redstone is done! Try it out by placing payment in the top chest. The same number of for-sale items should pop out of the dropper. If you have any problems, go back and check each step carefully. Look out for the way repeaters and comparators point, and how redstone torches are placed (on a block's top, or on the side of a block).

27. Now you can decorate your vending machine. In front of the dropper, place a block of your choice. Decorate it with an item frame and a chicken. The items from the dropper will still pop through to the front of this.

28. Place a wall behind the chest and beside the dropper's decoration to hide the redstone. Add signs to explain what customers should do.

29. Keep decorating until you are satisfied. I've made a store around the vending machine. I used orange and white wool, light-gray stained glass panes, spruce wood blocks, and an acacia wood door. (Plus lots of item frames with roast chicken in them!) In the back, I've enclosed all the redstone in a maintenance area with spruce wood. Inside, there are stairs so you can easily get to the dropper to add goods and to the chest to collect your payment!

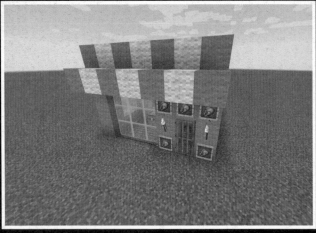

GREAT STORIES FOR MINECRAFTERS

Check out these unofficial Minecrafter adventures from Sky Pony Press!

Invasion of the Overworld

MARK CHEVERTON

Battle for the Nether

MARK CHEVERTON

Confronting the Dragon

MARK CHEVERTON

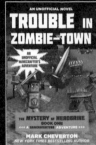

Trouble in Zombie-town

MARK CHEVERTON

The Quest for the Diamond Sword

WINTER MORGAN

The Mystery of the Griefer's Mark

WINTER MORGAN

The Endermen Invasion

WINTER MORGAN

Treasure Hunters in Trouble

WINTER MORGAN

Available wherever books are sold!